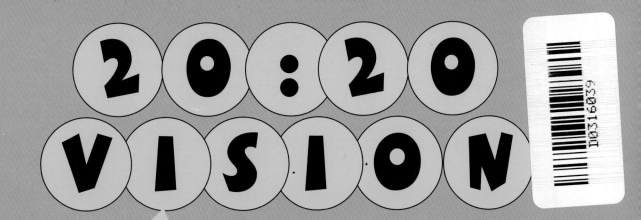

20:20 VISION

Prepare for lift-off!

Hi there! I'm Ray Galactica and I'd like to welcome you to *20:20 Vision.* Like all good space cadets, you'll need eagle eyes for this spectacular issue of *The Navigator*, which is all about taking a good look at things and learning from them. On my mission I'll show you some marvellous magnified microbes, and give you the chance to reflect on exactly how mirrors work. You can also go back in time to Ancient Greece to experience a mouth-watering menu. Warning: the wild hedgehog may give you indigestion!

Beam me up!

Text Type	Literacy Skills	Wider Curriculum Links
Report (visual)	Making comparisons; expressing and justifying opinions	**History** Unit 12: How did life change in our locality in Victorian times?
Recount (visual)	Comparing and contrasting information; language analysis	**History** Unit 11: What was it like for children in Victorian Britain?
Report/ Persuasive	Interpreting information; making judgments	**History** Units 14 and 15: Who were the Ancient Greeks? How do we use Ancient Greek ideas today?
Report/ Persuasive	Information retrieval; linking text and visuals	**Geography** Unit 15: The mountain environment
Report	Information retrieval; comparing information; expressing and justifying opinions	**Science** Unit 6B: Micro-organisms
Explanation	Summarising information	**Science** Unit 6F: How we see things
Explanation/ Instructional	Summarising information; comparing and contrasting information; understanding authorial intent	**Science** Unit 6F: How we see things
Report/ Instructional	Interpreting information; language analysis	**Art and Design** Unit 6A: People in action
Report	Summarising information; information retrieval	**Art and Design** Unit 6B: What a performance
Report	Close reading; summarising information	**Art and Design** Unit 6B: What a performance
Fun Spread		
		ICT: Year 6 Schemes of Work

DIFFERENCE

Life in Britain has changed a great deal over the last hundred years or so. The places we live in have changed too. These pictures show a town in the 1890s, and the same town today.

A CENTURY MAKES...

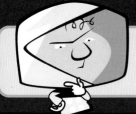

How many differences can you spot?

A WEEK IN THE LIFE

What would it be like to live in Victorian times? Your lifestyle would depend on whether you were male or female, and how well off your parents were. Here is a week in the very different lives of three children, all born on the same day – 2 February 1870.

MONDAY

Billy

"Food and clothes and a place to sleep. Must be better than life sweeping the streets and sleeping rough."

On his tenth birthday, Billy joined the army.

Lizzy

"It's hard to leave. But Mum'll have one less mouth to feed."

On her tenth birthday, Lizzy went into service.

Julia

"It is nice to have a party for my birthday."

On her tenth birthday, Julia had a party.

TUESDAY

Billy & Lizzy

On Tuesday, the recruits marched to their training camp.

"No one near my age, except those boys in front, who aren't friendly. And my feet hurt. Still, I expect it'll get better."

"It's only noon and I'm tired out! I've been up since five. How can a family of five make so much washing-up?"

On Tuesday, Lizzy began her new duties.

Julia

"I am SO bored! To think I am expected to live like this for the rest of my life."

On Tuesday, Julia went visiting with her mother.

WEDNESDAY

Billy

"I never saw so many potatoes in my entire life! Do I really have to peel them all?"

On Wednesday, Billy settled in at his new camp.

Lizzy

"I thought I knew how to peel potatoes. But no. I don't peel them Cook's way."

On Wednesday, Lizzy made Mrs Green, the cook, angry.

Julia

"I wish I could just dig my heels in and ride fast. But no. Mama says I have to ride 'like a lady'."

On Wednesday, Julia rode in the park with her mother.

THURSDAY

Billy

'Left, right! Left, right!' I'd rather be peeling spuds! But at least I'm fed and get a place to sleep.

On Thursday, Billy learned to march.

Lizzy & Julia

On Thursday, Julia had an early piano lesson.

It's very cold this morning. My fingers are cold even in my muff. I'll play the piano badly and the music master will scold me. That girl looks colder than I am. Why doesn't she wrap up?

This is the second time I've had to scrub these steps. I don't see what was wrong with them the first time! The water is SO cold.

On Thursday, Mrs Green was cross again.

FRIDAY

Billy

This is more like it. I feel more like a soldier now I have a uniform.

On Friday, Billy learned to beat the drum.

Lizzy

Well, thank goodness for that! She's not such a bad thing after all. I suppose she has to be strict with everyone to start with.

On Friday, Mrs Green was pleased with Lizzy.

Julia

This is lovely! What a shame acting is such a 'low' profession. I know I could never become an actress.

On Friday, Julia went to the theatre.

SATURDAY

Billy & Julia

On Saturday, Julia had lessons at home.

Here comes Miss Bailey. More lists of kings and queens and what goods are produced by the countries in the Empire! I wonder what part of the Empire those soldiers are off to?

I haven't even been here a week, and already I'm almost marching in step! It's very exciting to be sailing off to see the Empire.

On Saturday, Billy and the rest of the regiment marched to Dover.

Lizzy

This paste for cleaning the silver smells terrible! It makes my head ache. Still, Mrs Green says I can have a cup of tea when it's done.

On Saturday, Lizzy cleaned the silver.

SUNDAY

Billy

The sea is so rough. I feel SO sick. I wish I was dead. I wish I had never joined the army.

On Sunday, the army sailed away from Britain.

Lizzy

I've only been here a week. It seems like much, much longer. It isn't as horrid as I thought at first. It'll be all right.

On Sunday, Lizzy went to family prayers.

Julia

I'm bored. I don't know why Papa has to get everyone in here for prayers. My friend Claire says it's silly and old-fashioned.

On Sunday, Julia went to family prayers.

THEO'S TAKE-AWAY TAVERNA

SOUPS AND STARTERS

6 chalci

1. **Spartan black broth** (a classic dish made with pork stock, salt and vinegar)
2. **Red lentil soup** (our own recipe, made with lentils, onions, garlic, root vegetables and marjoram)
3. **Black pudding** (a spicy black sausage made with goats' blood)

MEAT DISHES

medium portion 10 chalci; large portion 1 obol

4. **Souvlakia** (tender pieces of lamb marinated in garlic, grape juice, olive oil and oregano and barbecued on skewers over a charcoal fire)
5. **Wild hedgehog stewed with lentils, leeks and carrots**
6. **Wild boar sausages** (our own recipe, mixed with onions, garlic and cumin)
7. **Roast thrush cooked with honey and served with milk cakes**
8. **Roast shoulder of mutton, flavoured with oregano and cumin**
9. **Mini game-bird roast** (choose from wood pigeon, owl, jackdaw or seagull)
10. **Ground game stew** (a spicy stew made with fresh seasonal game, including white-breasted marten, mole and cat)

FISH DISHES

medium portion 10 chalci; large portion 1 obol

11. **Salted Black Sea tunny fish braised with sour grapes**
12. **Savoro** (one of our house specialities: mackerel pickled in oil and vinegar with dill)
13. **Grilled red mullet marinated in olive oil, citron and fresh herbs**
14. **Fresh local octopus** (tenderised on rocks and cooked with white wine and garlic)
15. **Fried squid served in a black ink sauce**

VEGETABLE DISHES

5 chalci

16. **Cabbage with spinach and mint** (a crunchy dish of fresh green cabbage, cooked with onions, garlic, spinach, courgettes and mint)
17. **Braised lettuce** (fresh cos lettuce, cooked with sage and white wine)
18. **Theo's salad** (our house-speciality salad made with figs, olives, beans, lentils, chickpeas and leeks)

> *"Simple dishes that satisfy us as much as sumptuous feasts."*
> (Epicurus)

All dishes are prepared daily on our own premises and cooked to your order.

Free donkey delivery within five kilometres of the Parthenon.

Slave orders welcome.

Last orders three hours after sunset.

DESSERTS
6 chalci

19. **Honey and barley pudding** (a traditional dish made with pot barley, ewe's milk, yoghurt and toasted sesame seeds)

20. **Athenian cheesecake** (a classic recipe made with curd cheese, Attic honey, lemons and fresh mint)

21. **Dried figs with chopped almonds**

22. **Honey-glazed sesame balls** (rich sweetmeats made with sesame seeds and Attic honey)

EXTRAS
3 chalci

23. **Hummus** (our own recipe, made with chickpeas, lemon juice and sesame oil)

24. **Olives in brine**

25. **Barley bread**

26. **Fresh or dried figs**

DRINKS

27. **Our own house barley wine** — *8 chalci*
28. **Scented wine** — *krater 2 obols; half-krater 1 obol*
    (Chios or Lesbos)

MEZE
2 obols

29. **Choose from our meze selection** (any five dishes for 2 persons)
    Edible iris bulbs • Truffles • Smoked fish Mushrooms • Sea urchins • Pigs' brains Snails • Grasshoppers • Crickets Peacock eggs • Artichokes

SPECIAL SET MENU FOR TWO PERSONS
1 drachma

Grilled frogs' legs

Roast pig stuffed with thrushes, ducks, figs and oysters

Braised lettuce

Pitta bread

Honey cheesecake

Figs with almonds

MOUNTAIN HOME

Welcome to the first brochure of the brand new Andorran ski resort, Mountain Home. At Mountain Home we have the perfect facilities for veteran skiing enthusiasts and newcomers alike.

ABOUT THE COUNTRY

Andorra is a small principality situated in the eastern Pyrenees between France and Spain – less than 500 square kilometres in size but with superb skiing, duty-free shopping, and après-ski. There are restaurants, bars and clubs in abundance. The main language is Catalan, but Spanish, French and English are widely spoken.

FRANCE

ANDORRA

SPAIN

THE MOUNTAIN HOME SKI SCHOOL

The Mountain Home Ski School is one of the finest in Europe. All the instructors speak English and possess international teaching qualifications. Classes are small (no more than six people at a time) and beginners are well supervised. The school operates five-day courses of three hours a day. If required, private tuition can be arranged for as little as £16 per hour. A highly efficient lift system carries experienced skiers up to the high, open slopes for long cruising runs, while the gentle nursery slopes are close to the centre.

SKI RESORT
Home from home – with snow!

CHALETS

Like everything else at Mountain Home, our centrally-heated wooden chalets are brand new and top-of-the-range. We have three chalet types to suit all needs, budgets and tastes. Chalets house a minimum of ten guests (maximum sixteen). Homey and Ultra chalets have a resident 'chalet host', who ensures that all needs and requirements are met.

Traditional
Basic but comfortable, with all the essentials: fully equipped kitchen, bathroom with shower, TV, etc.

Homey
As the name suggests, comfortable and friendly. All the amenities of Traditional chalets, with 'homey' extras. The bathroom contains a bath as well as a shower, for instance, and the TV is larger, with a DVD player.

Ultra
Absolute luxury, with all those little extras, including whirlpool bath, balcony and open fires. You name it, Ultra has it.

MEALS
Unless otherwise requested, all cooking in Homey and Ultra chalets is done by the resident chalet host, whose culinary expertise is guaranteed to satisfy.

SNOWBOARDING

Andorra is fast becoming *the* European centre for snowboarding enthusiasts. An experience like no other, this 'coolest' of modern winter sports is a cross between surfing and skateboarding. Don't worry if you've never done either – full tuition is provided and all necessary equipment is available for short-term hire. We have a special fun snowboard park, with superb powder descents and jumps. This you have to try!

SKI AND SNOWBOARD PACKS
Rental prices in pounds sterling per person

	Adult	Child under 14
Number of days	5	5
Skis and Poles	35	25
Boots	18	12
Lift pass	90	FREE
Ski / Snowboard Tuition	65	55
Snowboard and Boots	55	45

MICRO-MARVELLOUS!
Looking at micro-organisms

Micro-organisms (also known as microbes) are tiny living things that are too small to see. They may be animals, plants or fungi. Such miniscule organisms were not known to exist until microscopes were invented.

Below are six micro-organisms that have been greatly magnified and six descriptions that tell you about them. Can you match each organism with the correct description?

USEFUL WORDS

bacterium – a tiny living thing made of one simple cell

cells – the tiny building blocks that make up living things

crustacean – a water-dwelling animal with a segmented body covered by a hard case

fungus – a living thing that takes its food from dead or decaying material or from the bodies of other living things

insect – a creature with three body parts, six legs and a pair of antennae

mite – a creature with a rounded body, eight short legs and no antennae

pollen – a powder which is made by flowers to fertilise other flowers of the same type

2

1

A. DUST MITE
- A kind of mite
- Measures 0.2 mm across
- Lives in houses, where it feeds on dust and flakes of human skin
- Has a hump-backed body covered in tiny grooves, and eight segmented legs with claws
- Body and legs are covered with sensitive hairs that pick up movements in the air

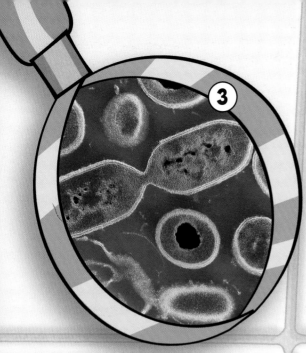

D. POLLEN GRAINS
• A fine dust produced by flowering plants.
Plants produce millions of pollen grains
• Each grain measures less than 0.05 mm across
• Pollen grains can be round, oval or spiky
• Carried on the breeze
from one flower
to another

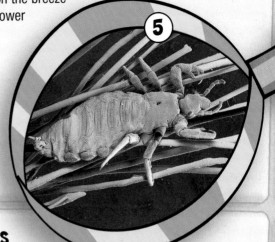

B. PIN MOULD
• A kind of fungus
• Measures about 0.2 mm across
• Found on old food or on plant or animal remains
• Forms a network of threads that feed on sugars
and starches in the food
• Looks like pinheads on stalks. The fungus
spreads when spores burst out of the pinheads

C. HEAD LOUSE
• A kind of insect
• Measures 3 mm long
• Lives in human hair. Holds on tightly to
the hair with its claws
• Uses its piercing, sucking mouthparts to
suck blood from the skin
• The female louse lays eggs, called nits,
and glues them to the base of hairs

E. CYCLOPS
• A tiny crustacean
• Measures 2 mm across
• Lives in fresh or salt water
• Has a single eye and two pairs of antennae.
The shorter pair are used to touch and smell its prey
• Drifts in the water or moves by kicking its feet and
flicking its long antennae
• Near the tail are two egg sacs, each
holding up to 50 eggs

F. LISTERIA
• A kind of bacterium
• Measures about
0.0001 mm across
• Listeria is rod-shaped.
Other bacteria are round,
or shaped like a comma
or a corkscrew
• Reproduces by copying the information inside
itself and then splitting in two. It can do this every 20 minutes
• Bacteria live in almost every habitat, including the human body.
Some bacteria are useful to us. Others are harmful and can
cause disease, and are often known as germs

Amazing mirrors

Have you ever watched a toddler looking in the mirror? She can't decide who is there! A toddler does not understand that the person in the mirror is a reflection of herself. She may try to look behind the mirror to see where the strange person is hiding!

How do mirrors work?

How do mirrors work?

A mirror produces a reflection because light bounces from its smooth shiny surface in a new direction. Our senses tell us that light travels in straight lines, so we see an image of the reflected object behind the mirror, where the light appears to have come from.

Mirror images

Mirror images

Your mirror image is almost identical to you, but not quite. The image is back-to-front. If you raise your right hand, your image appears to raise its left hand. If you hold some writing up to the mirror, the reflection is difficult to read. Can you read this writing? You can if you use a mirror!

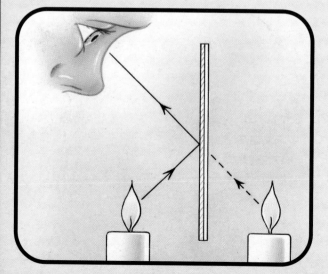

Hall of mirrors

The image in a flat mirror is the same size as the original. But curved mirrors produce distortion. In the hall of mirrors at the fairground, the curved mirrors magnify, shrink or invert (turn upside down) your image. You can see how you would look with legs like a giraffe and a head the size of a planet!

A convex mirror curves outwards

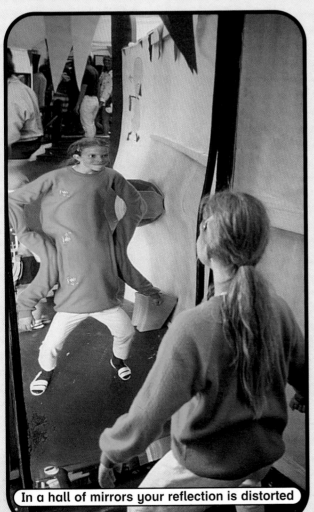

In a hall of mirrors your reflection is distorted

Convex and concave

Curved mirrors are not just fairground novelties. A convex mirror (one that bulges out in the middle like the back of a spoon) reflects a wider view than a flat mirror. Convex security mirrors allow shopkeepers to keep an eye on the whole store from behind the counter. A concave mirror (one that is hollow in the middle like the bowl of a spoon) produces a close-up magnified image. Concave mirrors are useful for shaving and putting on make-up.

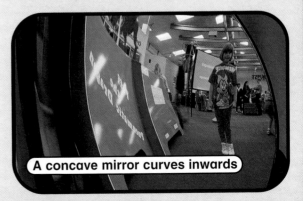

A concave mirror curves inwards

Mirror marvels

Mirror marvels

The expression 'It's all done with mirrors' is sometimes used to describe how magicians create their illusions. 'Pepper's ghost' is a theatre trick used to create the appearance of a ghostly figure. A brightly lit actor stands in a pit below the stage. The audience sees his reflection in a sloping sheet of glass that acts like an invisible mirror.

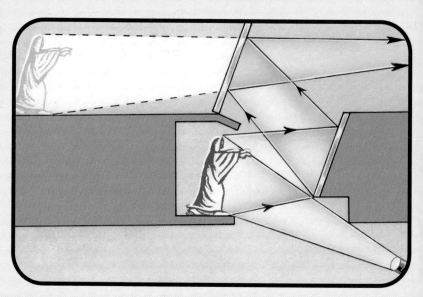

Clever kaleidoscopes

Clever kaleidoscopes

A kaleidoscope contains two mirrors at an angle of 60°. Pieces of coloured plastic between the mirrors make random patterns as the kaleidoscope is turned. The combined reflections in the pair of mirrors create an image with the same symmetry as a hexagon or a snowflake.

Mirrors inside a kaleidoscope create symmetrical patterns

Clone yourself!

Clone yourself!

Would you like to see an infinite number of copies of yourself? You can if you stand between two parallel mirrors.

Your image in the first mirror is reflected in the second mirror. The second image is reflected in the first mirror and so on. You see a line of images disappearing to infinity in both directions!

Periscopes

Periscopes

A submarine crew use a periscope to see above the water surface.
A periscope uses mirrors to change the direction of light to see over barriers
or around corners.

How to make a periscope

You will need:

- two small mirrors
- a tall narrow card box
- scissors
- sticky tape

1. Cut windows on opposite sides at the top and the bottom of the box as shown in the diagram.

2. Angle the mirrors with their reflecting surfaces facing each other as shown. Tape them into place.

3. Try using your periscope to look over a wall!

Don't drop this one!

Don't drop this one!

The world's most expensive mirror is in the Hubble space telescope. It uses a huge concave mirror that collects light from distant stars and galaxies. Using the space telescope, astronomers can see to the edge of the universe!

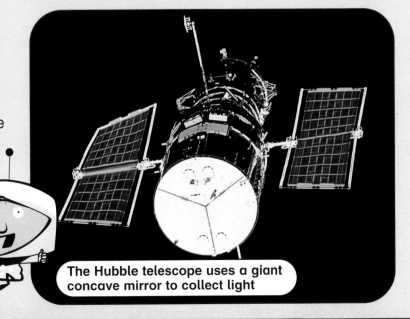

The Hubble telescope uses a giant concave mirror to collect light

Kan you do KARATE?

Karate is a Japanese martial art. The word 'karate' means 'empty hand', because people fight one another with their bare hands and feet. The history of the art stretches back for more than 500 years, when it was used by fighters who were forbidden to carry weapons. Today, it is practised as a form of self-defence. Karate is not easy to learn. It uses the whole body, and relies on high-energy punches, strikes and kicks. It requires hard work and concentration.

Ready for action

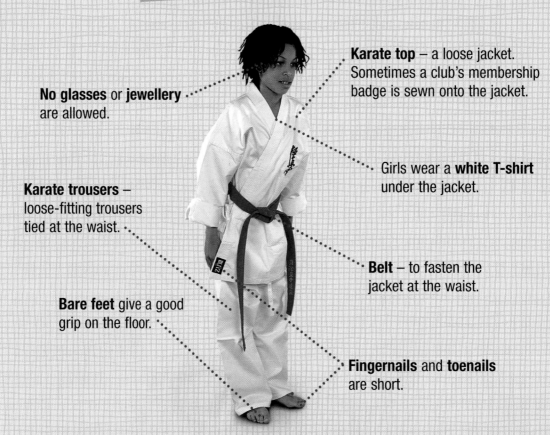

No glasses or **jewellery** are allowed.

Karate top – a loose jacket. Sometimes a club's membership badge is sewn onto the jacket.

Girls wear a **white T-shirt** under the jacket.

Karate trousers – loose-fitting trousers tied at the waist.

Belt – to fasten the jacket at the waist.

Bare feet give a good grip on the floor.

Fingernails and **toenails** are short.

Karate fighters bow to each other before each contest.

Karate awards

Every 3 to 6 months, karate students progress to a new grade. Each time they pass a grading, they receive a certificate and a new belt. The colour of the belt matches their grade.

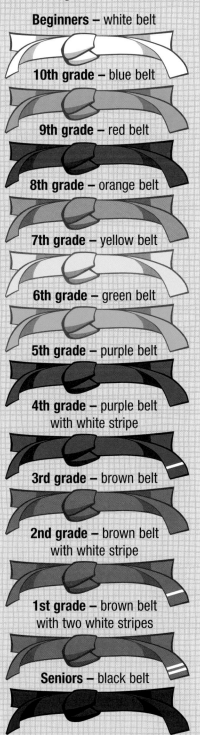

Beginners – white belt

10th grade – blue belt

9th grade – red belt

8th grade – orange belt

7th grade – yellow belt

6th grade – green belt

5th grade – purple belt

4th grade – purple belt with white stripe

3rd grade – brown belt

2nd grade – brown belt with white stripe

1st grade – brown belt with two white stripes

Seniors – black belt

Karate kicks

Karate kicks are more powerful than punches. There are four basic kinds of kick: the **front kick**, the **back kick**, the **side kick** and the **roundhouse kick**. The front kick (known by the Japanese name of *mae-geri*) uses the power of the hips to thrust the ball of the foot into an opponent's stomach!

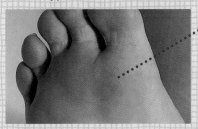

The ball of the foot is good for kicking because it is so hard. You could hurt yourself if you kicked with your toes.

How to perform a front kick

1 Stand in an upright position with your feet apart, and your left leg slightly forward. Bend your knees and hold your fists up to protect your face and body. Bring your right leg forward and raise the right knee high. Pull your toes up.

- *Pulling toes up prevents injury when you kick*

- *Supporting leg is bent*

- *Kicking knee is higher than the target*

2 Straighten your right leg by thrusting out the ball of your right foot. Then pull the kick back, and set your foot down carefully.

- *Left leg is bent*

- *Keep your fist up to defend your face*

- *Aim the kick towards target*

- *Kick with the ball of your foot. Never use your toes*

CLOWNING AROUND

Clowns have been around for thousands of years, in many cultures. The earliest clowns were 'court jesters' or 'fools', who were able to say and do things in court that even great lords couldn't have got away with. They could criticise and comment on the ruler's plans and ideas where others might not dare. Some clever jesters were able to use their unusual position — and their humour — to affect court policy. This must have made them pretty unpopular with more serious courtiers and advisers!

2500 BC
The earliest known jester was at the court of Egyptian pharaoh, Dadkeri-Assi.

1818 BC
Jesters are known to have clowned around in ancient China.

AD 1520
This is when jesters were first seen by Europeans at the court of Montezuma, the Aztec king.

FAMOUS JESTERS

Nasir Ed Din

One day the King looked in the mirror and decided that he wasn't as pretty as he used to be — and started crying. Wanting to keep in with the King, his courtiers also burst into tears. When the King stopped crying so did everyone else — except Nasir the jester. When the King asked him why he was still crying, Nasir answered, "Sire, you looked at yourself in the mirror for just a moment and you cried. I have to look at you all the time!"

Yu Sze

Around 300 BC, a Chinese emperor named Shih Huang-Ti was supervising the construction of the Great Wall of China. It was dangerous work, and thousands of labourers died during the building. When the Wall was finished, Shih Huang-Ti gave orders for it to be painted. Even though this would almost certainly have resulted in many more deaths, the only person to speak out against the plan was the Emperor's fool, Yu Sze. Through humour, he persuaded the Emperor not to have the Wall painted after all. Because so many lives were saved by his boldness, Yu Sze is a national hero of modern China.

Robert Armin

He was an Elizabethan actor-fool in William Shakespeare's theatre company. Armin wrote a book about famous fools — one of the first histories of clowning.

DID YOU KNOW?

The actor who played the fool in Shakespeare's plays was allowed to 'ad-lib' (put in his own unscripted jokes and dialogue). Often these ad-libs were about current affairs. When they went down well with the audience, the ad-libs were often added to the script. This practice continues to the present day.

THE FIRST CIRCUS CLOWN

The first English circus was created by Philip Astley in 1768. The first clown to appear at this circus called himself Billy Buttons. As the circus became more popular, Astley employed other clowns. Their acts were generally based on Billy Buttons' routines. Such routines are still used in circuses today.

CLOWN SCHOOLS

Just as there are schools for dancers, actors and singers, there are schools for adults and children who fancy their chances as circus performers. Some schools offer full-year training; others offer short workshops. Circus schools claim that the skills they teach develop the students' mind, body, and creative spirit, and boost confidence and self-esteem. Full-time circus schools for children teach general subjects (Maths, English, Science, etc.) as well as circus skills. What a pity ordinary schools don't teach circus skills. School life would be so much more fun!

Skills taught at circus schools include tightrope walking, juggling, unicycling, stilt walking, clowning, acrobatics, balloon modelling, magic and mime.

Most circus schools offer specialist courses for clowns. Approaches vary, but a typical 12-month programme might look something like this.

- The first term would focus on general skills.
- In the second term there would be greater emphasis on the creation of original material and image. Costume and make-up would be studied in detail, as would the use of props and equipment.
- The final term would most likely concentrate on rehearsals and appearances in actual venues, such as hospitals, community centres and schools.

FEMALE CLOWNS

There are very few records of female clowns. One of the earliest-known female clowns was Amelia Butler, who toured in the 1850s with two circuses: Kemp's Mammoth English Circus and Nixon's Great American Circus.

A modern female clown — Risa Roberta Goldberg — gives some wonderful insights into her life. Once she decided to become a clown, Risa bought a box of special make-up, borrowed a clown suit with ruffles at the neck, wrists and ankles, and started playing the fool in public.

After various attempts to make a living as a clown, Risa became Risa the Musical Clown (she plays a number of instruments), hiring herself out as a singing telegram, funny greetings card, and for balloon deliveries with music. In order to get more used to her clown character, she put on her costume and make-up and walked around town, stood on street corners waving at cars, and did musical shows at local libraries. She also started taking professional clown classes in magic, juggling, balloon twisting, and face painting.

"When I put on my face and costume," Risa says, "everyone wants to know me, shake my hand, get my autograph. Cars sound their horns, people follow me, little kids stare in awe. In fifteen years of clowning around, I've clowned on planes, boats, trains, at the beach and in parks. Now I have a van to hold all my gear and I'm teaching others to be clowns. I've even launched my mother as a clown!"

On your bike

When you're out cycling, you need to know what road signs mean. They give a lot of useful information that can help you to avoid getting into difficult and dangerous situations. Some road signs warn about things that are going on ahead; others tell you about speed limits and other rules of the road.

Signs giving warning are usually in a red triangle.
Signs giving orders are usually in a red circle.
Signs giving positive instructions are usually in a blue circle.

What do you think these road signs are telling you?

1
(a) Road works
(b) Man putting up umbrella
(c) Pizza restaurant ahead

2
(a) Thomas the Tank Engine and Friends
(b) Level crossing without barrier or gate ahead
(c) Train spotters ahead

3
(a) No cyclists allowed
(b) Cycle route ahead
(c) Cycle rally

4
(a) No cyclists allowed
(b) Cycle route ahead
(c) Leave your car and ride a bike

5
(a) Bad driver ahead
(b) Slippery road
(c) Formula 1 track

6
(a) Traffic queues likely ahead
(b) Drivers playing follow my leader ahead
(c) Car park

7
(a) Bus lane
(b) No buses
(c) Cheap buses

8
(a) Amphibious cars only
(b) Quayside or river bank
(c) Swimming allowed

Some signs warn about animals that may be in the road

Cattle

Wild animals

Wild horses or ponies

Accompanied horses or ponies

The Highway Code lists all the rules of the road for drivers, motorcyclists, cyclists, and pedestrians. It says 'You MUST obey all traffic signs and traffic light signals.'

Do you know the sequence when traffic lights change colour? Do they go:

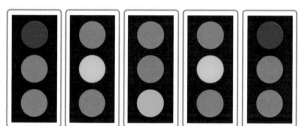

Red – amber – green – amber – red?

OR

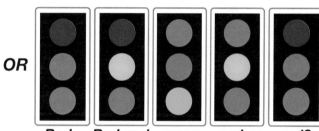

Red – Red and – green – amber – red?
amber

What do the colours tell you to do?

The Highway Code also says that cyclists should wear a cycle helmet at all times; light-coloured or fluorescent clothing to help other road users see them in daylight and poor light; reflective clothing or accessories such as armbands in the dark.

Do you know any of the other rules for cyclists in The Highway Code?

Cycling can be dangerous because there is so much traffic on the roads nowadays. The National Cycle Network, a Millennium project, will make cycling safer. When it is finished, 16 000 kilometres of cycle track will link towns and countryside all over Britain.

Byte-Sized ICT

Mountain Home ski resort

ICT: Unit 6a
Multimedia
presentation

Dream ticket

Wow! Doesn't skiing look fantastic! Why not create a multimedia presentation using text, images and sound based on the brochure on pages 10 and 11. You can also include some details on how to travel to Andorra.

Your presentation needs to be really persuasive so that people will choose to book a holiday at Mountain Home ski resort. You can also do some research and include some interesting facts about Andorra, and fascinating facts about skiing.

Remember to check your presentation carefully, and make sure your links work as well.

Amazing mirrors (part 1)

Funny faces

You have seen some of the weird and wonderful ways a mirror can distort images, on pages 14 to 17. Computers offer other ways of distorting and changing images – to improve them, to make them interesting, funny or just plain odd!

Take some photos of yourself or a friend on a digital camera and use software to change them in unusual ways. You could stretch them so that you look very short and fat, or turn yourself into wallpaper.

The great thing about doing it on the computer is that if you don't like it, you can always go back to your original photo file and start again! Go on – get snapping!

Amazing mirrors (part 2)

ICT: Unit 6d Using the Internet

Hubble telescope research challenge

What can you find out about the Hubble telescope? Search for information on the Internet about Hubble using a 'search engine'. Try just typing in the word 'Hubble'. How many results do you get? You will probably find you need to refine your search a bit more. Think about how you could narrow it down. Try to find at least two child-friendly sites with useful information about Hubble.

Helpful hint!

Search engines are websites that allow you to key in a word or words, and then they search the web for websites containing those words.

What a difference a century makes ...

Town table

How many differences did you find, on pages 4 and 5, between the town in the 1890s and today? You could use a word-processor to type a list. A good way to set this out clearly would be to use a table.

You will need to use two columns, one for the Victorian town and one for the town today. On one side you can type what feature you notice, and on the other side, type how it is different. The number of rows in your table will depend on how many differences you find! Most software will allow you to add rows afterwards if you spot some more as you go along. Don't forget you will need a row for the headings of your columns too!

Victorian town	MODERN TOWN

Helpful hint!

Why not use an old-fashioned font for the Victorian town and a more modern one for today? You should be able to highlight the column to allow you to change only the text on that side.

Clowning around

Design-a-clown

Design the best-dressed clown in town! Use an art or graphics program on your computer to design the costume and makeup for your clown. Think carefully about using bright, contrasting colours and wacky patterns. You could use the 'fill' tool to fill in an outline with a certain pattern or colour. It is normally shown by a bucket icon.

If possible, use an object-based program, which allows you to move and manipulate each item that you draw as a separate object. This means you can change your mind and try out different ideas more easily.

This is the bucket icon.

On your bike

Cycle safely

Did you know all the signs and safety points for cyclists on pages 24 and 25? Design a cycle safety leaflet using publishing software (or a word-processor) to appeal to children of your age.

It will need to show all the important points, but in an interesting and eye-catching way. A bit of humour may make it more appealing and memorable. Perhaps you could include a cartoon with a speech bubble?

You could also think about making it into a folding leaflet. Your software may have a 'wizard', allowing you to type each 'page' in the right place on your A4 sheet.

If you are pleased with the results, why not ask to print some to give out to any keen cyclists in your class?

Glossary

abundance	a plentiful supply of something
accessories	extra items
amenities	things that add to your comfort, ease or pleasure
amphibious	able to live or move in water and on land
après-ski	the evening, especially its social activities, following a day's skiing
Attic honey	honey from Athens
braised	meat or vegetables cooked by browning in fat and then stewing in a covered pot
broth	a thin soup made with meat, fish or vegetable juices
courtiers	the servants or officials in the court of a king or queen
culinary	to do with the kitchen, food or cooking
fluorescent	giving out a hard bright light
ground game	animals that live on the ground and can be caught to eat
identical	exactly equal or the same
infinity	endless space and time, impossible to measure or calculate
jackdaw	a small grey-headed crow, often noted for its curiosity

labourers	people who do heavy work
marinated	softened before cooking by soaking in a sauce
marten	a weasel-like carnivore
microscopes	instruments that make very small objects look larger
miniscule	tiny
periscope	an instrument made of mirrors and a tube used to see something that is above you or out of your sight
principality	a state ruled by a prince
routine	a set sequence in a performance
segmented	arranged into segments or sections
spore	a seed or germ cell that separates from its parent before it begins to develop
sweetmeat	an archaic word for a sweet
truffle	a strong-smelling fungus found underground that is eaten as a delicacy
tuition	teaching
veteran	someone who has been doing something for a long time and has a lot of experience at it

Index